CREATIVE THINKING

Problem Solving Across the Curriculum

Ages 8-10

Activities and ideas to develop a creative perspective
in problem solving across the curriculum

Ann Baker

CONTENTS

INTRODUCTION

Adults accept that problems will occur at home or at work, and that they need the disposition, skills and strategies to deal with them. Children need to be given opportunities to identify exactly what the presented problem is, and shown creative strategies to help them solve it and persist with challenging situations.

Creativity is at the heart of learning. Children are more resilient in their learning when they are absorbed, focused and challenged in the activities they undertake. Problem solving and investigations across the curriculum require a creative perspective, which involves all three of these personal attitudes to learning.

The activities in this book present a wide range of problematic situations for which there is more than one solution or more than one approach to the solution. In real life, problems are not usually neatly presented nor are the solutions immediately visible. When a potential solution is found, it needs to be evaluated to see if it is the best solution possible. Creative thinking illustrates a flexibility of thought, which allows us to consider a variety of approaches to a problem.

These activities will lay the foundation skills, strategies and disposition needed for children to become lifelong problem solvers and versatile learners.

ABOUT THIS BOOK

TEACHERS' FILE
The teachers' file offers advice on how to make the most of this book. It defines the different types of problems presented and how children can benefit from using them. It contains ideas for classroom organisation as well as background notes, ICT tips, assessment ideas and suggestions for parental involvement.

QUICK STARTS
This section offers activity and game ideas that help to promote a community of problem solvers and creative thinkers who will take a risk, come up with ideas, and develop problem solving strategies and the disposition to persevere. These activities require little or no preparation and can be used across various learning areas to complement existing lesson plans.

ACTIVITY BANK
The activity bank contains 27 photocopiable activities that cover creative thinking and problem solving skills relating to mathematics, visual literacy, music and dance, values and communication. The activities can be used in any order and can be used by children working individually or in groups.

CHALLENGES
These photocopiable task cards offer creative investigational challenges. They can be given to individual pupils or groups, and they can be used at any time and in any order. The tasks have the potential to become extended projects where pupils will share, present and develop a wide range of communication skills.

HOW TO USE THIS BOOK

QUICK STARTS

What if the sound on the TV faded?

For this activity the pupils work with a partner to present a TV clip (from the news, a documentary or soapy that everyone is familiar with). The catch is that they have no volume. Their lips may move but no noise comes out. Encourage the use of facial gestures and hand or body movements to get the message across. Explain to the pupils that this is not a mime. Can the class follow the clip? Why/why not?

Quick Starts are ideal warm-up activities for the beginning of a lesson. Each activity is intended to provide 10-15 minutes of group or whole class discussion. Reflect on the completed task with the children. Ask what they learned and whether there was anything that surprised them.

Example

'What if the Sound on the TV faded?' (page 15) encourages the pupils to explore visual communication only through body movement and facial expression. This activity can be extended to include discussions on how we show our different emotions through our body language and the impact this can have on our relationships with others.

ACTIVITY BANK

These photocopiable activities can be used by individuals, groups or the whole class. They could provide the focus for a whole lesson. The activities will not in themselves achieve the objectives, but they will make children start to think about these often complex issues and strategies. Whilst some of the activities have a problem solving focus, they are all designed to encourage pupils to think creatively. By becoming flexible, versatile, open-minded learners, they will develop the skills to think more objectively and laterally in their investigations and in the solutions to problems.

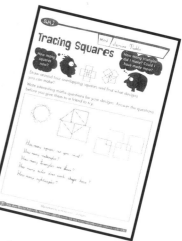

Example

'Tracing Squares' (PCM 3, Page 20) asks the pupils to investigate the different shapes created by four overlapping squares and to create a series of questions from their investigations for other members of the class to consider. Encourage them to identify a methodology for recording the number of different 2D shapes and their properties. What would happen if the number of squares were increased to eight?

CHALLENGES

These photocopiable activities are perfect for use in learning centres, in the school library or in the classroom. The investigational nature of the activities is in line with National Curriculum requirements and supports the development of investigational problem-solving skills.

Example

'Chinese Whispers' (Task Card 1, Page 46) explores speaking and listening skills, short-term memory and concentration. With practice, it is possible to memorise accurately longer messages – who can correctly and accurately communicate the longest message to a friend? Ask the pupils to create other strategies for improving their ability to listen and to speak clearly and confidently.

TEACHERS' FILE

Characteristics of the problems

There are five different types of problems presented in this book:

- Mathematical problems—focus on using estimation, efficient number strategies, shape and position with flexibility and strategic thinking.
- Visual literacy problems—focus on using elements of visual language (colour, position, shape and planning) to convey ideas, create mood and develop visual flexibility and creativity.
- Music and dance problems—focus on developing perceptions about the ways in which rhythm, pattern, sound and movement can be combined to create solutions to musical challenges.
- Values problems—focus on reflecting and evaluating responses to everyday problem situations where interpersonal or ethical decisions need to be made. They provide an opportunity for philosophical thinking.
- Communication problems—focus on communicating clearly through spoken and written language specific to the task, purpose and audience.

Planning for creative thinking

Pupils at this level often don't want to take risks or to present in front of the class. By using open-ended problems and creating a strong sense of learning community, they will:

- take a risk and think creatively with minimum focus on the right answer (as often there isn't one)
- offer ideas to their peers, and listen and accept their peers' ideas without judgement
- think critically and reflect on ideas and strategies they and others use, to become skilful and strategic problem solvers (keeping a journal would be useful)
- consider the contributions they make to a group
- participate fully in discussions and presentations
- become responsible and reciprocal learners.

CLASSROOM ORGANISATION

Building creative thinking into the week

Pupils in the middle years can become disconnected from school activities. The problems in this book are topical and of interest to this age group. Through the open-ended problems pupils can bring their own experiences and interests to solving and presenting solutions. Fun is central to the activities but academic perseverance is also required. The pupils will become engaged in critical, creative, reflective and empathetic thinking which will enhance the weekly programme. The problems can be stand-alone, the focus of specific curriculum areas or integrated within the existing weekly plan.

Communication problems—focus on pupils getting their ideas across in a number of different ways and this will blend into many curriculum areas.

Visual Literacy problems—focus on elements of art appreciation and critical literacy, integrating effectively into literacy or critical literacy lessons and media or art lessons.

Mathematics problems—complement the normal maths programme.

Values problems—reflect typical pupil issues that may arise in the week or are seen in youth culture or current world issues.

Music, **Dance** and **Visual Literacy** problems—integrate and blend easily into the weekly programme.

CLASSROOM ORGANISATION

Learning styles

We all use a variety of audio, visual and kinaesthetic approaches to support our learning. This book covers a broad range of learning styles. Pupils will respond verbally, mathematically, visually, dramatically and musically to the problems. They will need to think logically and systematically and respond creatively and flexibly, to solve problems and make their presentations. They will also be reflective and philosophical, and can respond kinaesthetically to act out and construct solutions. Most of the intelligences identified by Howard Gardner are addressed through the activities, for instance, when solving:

mathematical problems – pupils will interpret verbal and visual information, estimate, explain, represent, justify and present solutions

visual literacy problems – pupils will interpret and respond to visual and design elements, emotionally, critically and creatively through a range of media

music and dance problems – pupils will use rhyme, rhythm, tone and mood to interpret and create new forms of music and choreography

values problems – pupils will listen carefully, be empathetic and consider others' perspectives, before responding visually or verbally

communication problems – pupils will generate ideas and consider audience and purpose as they get those ideas across.

As the pupils work on and present their solutions, they will be simultaneously using several intelligences or learning styles. This reflects the real world where one intelligence is rarely used in total isolation from the others.

Equipment

Equipment needed is either readily available cheaply or is gathered from recycling everyday objects and materials. Try to ensure that pupils have access to:

- scrap paper
- paper
- scissors
- pencils
- coloured pencils or felt pens
- shapes (plastic or card templates)
- playdough
- googly eyes (optional)
- drinking straws or popsticks
- coloured chalks
- glue
- scrap materials such as boxes, Kitchen roll cylinders, ice-cream containers
- counters in two colours
- tape measures
- scales
- bottle tops

Planning activities

Pupils need to be given time, space and encouragement to persist when the going gets tough, retrace their steps or try a different tack. They need to know there is enough time to work through what seems a mess, organise themselves or break a task into small manageable steps. They also need the benefit of working with peers.

When planning the weekly schedule, allocate time, space and technologies required for the problem solving, and for the practice and presentation of solutions. You may need to include specific mini-lessons on problem solving strategies, such as Polya's model, explained here:

See: What is this problem about? What is it asking me to do? What information am I given/do I need?

Plan: How can I get started? How can I make this manageable? What have I done like this before?

Do: This is how I actually collect, analyse, interpret and represent information and strategies for critical and creative thinking.

Check: How effective were we? What will we do next time?

Presenting

Giving and watching presentations are an important feature of the problems in this book, so you may need to:

- negotiate and agree on rules for watching and listening to presentations and giving positive feedback
- review and extend strategies for getting and holding audience attention
- review multi-media options that can be used (props, visual images, sound effects, digital technologies)
- discuss timelines and expectations for presentations
- set acceptable parameters for choreography and words for songs
- encourage all pupils to find a way of contributing to the group presentations (even if it is simply making props).

Sharing and reflecting

To be successful open-ended problem solvers and presenters, pupils need a safe and supportive classroom space where they can be a community of learners who feel confident taking risks, make mistakes and feel supported by peers. The following questions will assist you to create such an environment:

- Is the classroom set-up comfortable for group work?
- Will the pupils have a choice of whom they work with?
- Can Socratic circles be easily set up for open forums or discussions?
- Are the resources ready and accessible?
- Is there a space where products can be displayed?
- Are there displays showing strategies for group work, active listening and quality presentations?
- Is there room for pupils to move around?
- Is there a quiet area?

Creative thinking strategies

Many middle years primary pupils are experienced with right answer only type questions and not open-ended problems. Suddenly being asked to be creative and take a risk could be difficult for them. Pupils at this age may become embarrassed when asked to do musical or dance presentations. You may need to model or scaffold various stages of the problem solving and presentation, and offer support as pupils:

- discover there is no exact prescription or right solution for the problem
- feel frustrated not knowing how to start or what to do
- run out of strategies to apply to the situations
- get stuck using a guess and check approach that 'fails' and don't know how to use information they've gathered
- try to make sense of the strategies, approaches and ideas of others
- learn about cooperation
- plan and rehearse a presentation.

iCT TiPS

General

There are many ways in which technology can be used to accompany the actual problem solving and to present or record performances. As the pupils work, there will be scope to use simple drawing programs, scan images into Word documents and capture photographic images as accompaniments to the solutions requiring procedures. Audio recorders or video cameras can be used as a part of the music and dance solutions. The actual performances can be recorded for reflection and later evaluation.

Interactive whiteboards

If you are fortunate enough to have access to an interactive whiteboard, you will be able to demonstrate to the whole class how some of the software listed above can be used. You can also use it to show pre-recorded presentations, and to freeze-frame and take closer looks at aspects of them. You can scan and present items of pupil work to involve the class in feedback and annotations on the work.

Software

There are many software packages that can be introduced to and used effectively by pupils in the Middle Primary years.

Kid Pix provides a drawing program and a stamp facility that can enhance the problem solving in many ways. The stamp facility for instance would allow pupils to create their own versions of 'the picnic'. The shapes available could be used to create 'shape tracing squares'. The ability to quickly draw lines would enable pupils to create their own gameboards and the free drawing facility has possibilities for many of the problems presented. Pupils with fine motor difficulties benefit from using these programs when problem solving.

Thinking With Pictures is an excellent mind mapping software package that can be used when brainstorming at the beginning of the problem solving process. It can also be used to enhance the thinking and writing involved in the communication problems.

Photo Simple is very easy-to use software that allows digital photos to be manipulated at the click or drag of the mouse. Photo Simple comes with its own built-in wizard that guides you step by step through every process as the photo story is created. It is possible to zoom in, zoom out, take a different perspective and create stories, sequences or procedures as in 'what's inside an egg' or 'make a bird' and add voice over or music-over.

PowerPoint, Paint programs and Word programs can all be used in conjunction with the problem solving to present solutions in a variety of formats.

Interactive whiteboards come with their own software such as Smart Ideas and the Smart Notebook. These can also be used effectively to present solutions.

Video and Audio Equipment

Schools often have video cameras, digital cameras and audio recorders available. Many of the problems presented in this book offer opportunities to capture pupil activity and performances. Parents can be invited to view segments at a special event. Pupils can become directors and mini-movie makers capturing each other's presentations. Editing packages such as Photo Simple make it easy to cut and overlay, images and sounds.

ASSESSMENT

Pupil assessment

As the pupils solve problems, it is possible to observe and record the strategies that they use. Some pupils will always stick to one approach, whereas others will try a variety of approaches. This gives you information not just about which strategies pupils use and how effectively they use them, but also information about how willing they are to take a risk and how flexibly they think.

Problem solving and creative thinking allows insights into pupil disposition, that is, how readily they begin thinking about the problem, how persistent they are in the face of a challenge and whether they have solving strategies. They may also favour a learning style they have a particular interest or talent in.

The different types of problems will also allow you to observe pupils as they work in a particular domain and to annotate work samples. The maths problems, for instance, allow mathematical information to be gained, such as: how reasonable their estimates are; what information they use to make them; and, what counting strategies they use to check their estimates. In the same way the other four types of problems will allow you to gain specific information related to the domain.

As the pupils work, you will be able to observe and note skills in:

- interpreting information
- drawing skills and effective use of colour and position
- working cooperatively with others to achieve a joint goal
- rhythm and tempo
- flexibility and stamina when performing dance sequences
- empathising with others
- and problem solving strategies and skills (of course).

Peer assessment

There will be many opportunities to engage in presenting and sharing, and peer assessment will be a part of the process. Encourage positive feedback where the pupils identify a part of the presentation or product that they thought was particularly effective or clever. Only after several positive comments should any constructive criticism be given. Model possible sentence starters for the constructive criticism so that feedback is in the form of, 'I would have liked to have heard some more about why you think some people are bullies and some are always the victims', rather than, 'You didn't explain ...'

Self-assessment

At each reflection, focus on one aspect, such as:
- cooperation
- persistence
- product
- strategies; ask the pupils to think about what they did well or found easy, and what they didn't do so well or found hard. Encourage the pupils to take responsibility for thinking about ways in which they might improve for next time.

PARENT INVOLVEMENT

Explain to parents that the pupils will work on open-ended problems requiring them to find solutions and create presentations. The goal is to link this to real-life problems that adults deal with each day. Ask parents to involve their children in some problem solving situations, for example, how to schedule the weekend's events that have set times and durations, and some of which overlap. This type of problem demonstrates skills in organisation and planning, and sharing of workload and responsibility so that everything gets done smoothly and on time.

Invite parents to celebrate the success of their children as problem solvers and creative thinkers by coming to presentations of solutions, products and performances.

PCM NOTES

PCM 1 Ask pupils to identify the emotions shown on the faces and describe the graph, noting how many pupils were surveyed. The pupils can then collect data to make their own emoticon graphs, and share and interpret each other's graphs.

PCM 2 Once pupils are confident playing the 'Buried Treasure' game, they should start thinking strategically about which coordinates eliminate most possibilities quickest. Suggest changing the game rules and creating a bigger map to explore winning strategies.

PCM 3 Ask pupils to investigate the overlapping shapes and then select for their questions. Model questions such as: 'What different shapes can be made by overlapping the squares?' 'What is the largest number of shapes that four overlapped squares can make?' Encourage the pupils to use a strategy for keeping track of the shapes counted.

PCM 4 Ask pupils to guess how many ants might be hidden under the sandwich or pie and why. What strategies work for quickly working out how many ants altogether? They might use their 9 and 6 times tables, or add 1 ant from each group of 6 to the group of 9 and add in 10s and 5s. Ask how many ants will go in the squares and why, before they begin.

PCM 5 Ask pupils to estimate the total value of the counters, then discuss the best way to work it out. Some strategies used will be; totalling the hands first then dividing the rest of the coins into smaller groups for counting and adding together later; counting all the similar values first and then add these subtotals later; and, doing multiplications based on how many of each type of counter. Reflect on which way works best, and why, before they create their counter picture.

PCM 6 The trees have been set out in blocks to make them easy to count. Help pupils to find clues that will eliminate some blocks easily, e.g. there is only one block in the NW corner. The clue about the owner with a quarter of the trees is difficult, so leave it until last. Pupils should plan and test their blocks and questions before swapping.

PCM 7 Review the stages of development inside an egg. Pupils should choose an animal that hatches from an egg such as a dinosaur, chicken or possibly a creature from a Harry Potter book. Explain that at first it will be difficult to identify, but as its features develop it becomes more obvious what creature will emerge.

PCM 8 Pupils should add more detail and colour to this 'blank canvas'. Talk about what colours, shapes and objects might be visible through the window, e.g. a crescent moon, owl's eyes, silhouette of a tree. Discuss what colours and features would make the room warm and inviting on a stormy night?

PCM 9 Review some positional language beforehand. Ask pupils which letters suit going through or under, or for standing on or sliding down. Some letters suggest certain activities, e.g. the letter 'C', which seems the ideal place to curl up and read a book.

PCM 10 Review the use of storyboards and different camera angles and shots. Discuss the possible reasons for selecting a particular shot for the first box. 'A close-up of Miss Muffett's happy face would contrast with a close-up of her frightened face in the last scene? Or 'Set the scene with a mid-shot so we know where she is and what she is doing.' Either would work equally well.

PCM 11 Pupils might first want to add more detail to the dog. Explain that each box must add something to the dog. They need to plan ahead what steps to add in each box. Encourage them to make the drawings visually clear. At the end, compare sequences and discuss how easy they are to follow.

PCM 12 Encourage pupils to cover the whole room with patterns. The pupils may prefer the striking effect of black-and-white and not add colour. If using colour, ask if the room is to be light and summery or dark and wintry. Or they could create a blue or a green room where tone is used to create depth.

PCM NOTES

PCM 13 Discuss the tricks that advertisers use to make their product appear better than others. Identify the untruths in the text and then discuss the kinds of colours advertisers would use for the packet and why. The pupils will then plan the colours and what to write and draw, to advertise the product truthfully.

PCM 14 Ask the pupils to talk about bullies and victims, then to share their views about the elephant. Pose one or two bullying scenarios and ask them how the victim might have avoided being bullied or got it to stop. They should then identify and explore a scenario.

PCM 15 Discuss why a chameleon does not want to be seen and why humans or other creatures might want to go unnoticed? Discuss making the fox blend into the picture, e.g. using a rust-coloured brick wall, some orangey flowers and a textured dirt floor (rub over a rough surface). Encourage pupils to experiment with art in the other boxes.

PCM 16 Explain that many people want something they don't have, but often if they get it, it is not what they wanted after all—just like the leopard. Ask the pupils why being plain is not appropriate for a leopard. Then they will complete the story to demonstrate the moral.

PCM 17 Discuss the embarrassing moment shown in the picture. How could this situation be less embarrassing? Ask pupils to share some embarrassing moments and ask them to suggest how they could have made it more or less embarrassing at the time.

PCM 18 Place pupils into groups of three and ask them to move smoothly through the letters YMCA, making each letter with their bodies. Demonstrate what is meant by jerky moves and smooth moves. Allow time for practise before they try it to music.

PCM 19 Ask some pupils to create opposite movements before explaining the rules of the dance. Allow time to practise sequences before they complete the page. Ask them to pick suitable music for their opposites dance. Once they have performed their dances, they can swap pages and try out each other's dances.

PCM 20 Review the Slip! Slop! Slap! sun safety rules with the pupils. Place them into groups to interpret the dance on the page before they create their own. Videotape their dances for presentation later.

PCM 21 Ask pupils to explain how the musical grid works. They should practise keeping the actions and the rhythm going before they invent their own human band. Enlarge or photocopy each musical grid so that the class can join in at the presentation.

PCM 22 The pupils can make and swap their own messages using this code rule. They can create their own continuous path on the second grid and use it to write the first message again.

PCM 23 When their bird is complete, the pupils can collect scrap materials, make a creature of their own and draw the steps for making it. A partner should follow the instructions to make a copy of the creature. Compare models and discuss the merits or weaknesses of the instructions.

PCM 24 Point out the materials in the garden and brainstorm other items useful for escaping. Pupils could name this very inventive dog. Suggest they draw the escape plan and add labels or captions.

PCM 25 Ask pupils why having questions in mind before reading helps the reader. Why are the suggested questions important ones? Allow time to compare their questions about Mad Dog and to say why some questions were the same and some were different.

PCM 26 Read the first story and ask why it is dull then read the next story and ask what makes it interesting. Ask pupils to think of an interesting situation they have experienced. They should then tell the story to a partner, who gives them feedback, then they should write it.

PCM 27 SMS messaging is popular with many young people who are very fast at it. Discuss the SMS shortcuts on the sheet and any others the pupils know. Write a longhand message to a friend, then show any SMS shortcuts that make it quicker to send.

QUICK STARTS

Active Graphs

Divide the class into similar-sized groups before going out into an open space. Give them a topic for graphing, for example 'Number of siblings'. Ask group 1 to organise themselves silently into lines according to the number of siblings in their family. Ask the class to describe the data set and to predict whether it will have the same or different distribution when group 2 joins. Ask them to explain their reasons. Repeat the process discussing changes each time until all groups have joined the line graph. Select other topics, such as 'Favourite flavour of chips'.

Guess my name

Ask the pupils to select a 2-D or 3-D shape and create clues for it. Clues need to go from least specific to most specific as in the example for a trapezium:

'This shape has four corners and four sides. Not all the sides are the same length. Only two sides are the same length. There are no right angles in my shape.'

Pupils can draw or note their thinking as the clues are presented.

Fill the Shape

Make large shapes (squares, triangles, rectangles, circles, irregular shapes) on the ground, each made from the same number of skipping ropes. Point out the lines (perimeters) enclosing the shapes are all the same length. Ask the pupils to predict how many people will fit into each shape and whether or not they will all fit the same number of people. Ask the pupils to explain their thinking before and after the shapes have been filled with people.

Pose a Problem

Apparently the hardest part of problem solving is posing the problem in the first place. Give the pupils an interesting topic and ask them to write a problem about that topic (you may never have to write a problem again). Model the process for an example such as 'the wind': When it is windy, hair goes everywhere. What could we do to keep our hair under control? Other topics could include: SMS messaging, radio stations, TV for young people, healthy food.

Square Puzzles

Begin with two identical squares. Place them onto an overhead projector, overlapping the two squares as you do so. Project the silhouette and ask the pupils what shape is made by the overlap. Ask them to explain their thinking each time you create a different overlap.

When the pupils are expert visualisers with two squares, move to three squares, or overlap other shapes.

Three Blind Mice: The ballet

Arrange the class into groups of four and ask them to create a ballet for 'Three Blind Mice' or any other nursery rhyme of their choice. You may have some budding ballet dancers who can teach a few basic moves. This is meant to be energetic and fun, so maybe it would be best done outside.

What if the sound on the TV faded?

For this activity the pupils work with a partner to present a TV clip (from the news, a documentary or soapy that everyone is familiar with). The catch is that they have no volume. Their lips may move but no noise comes out. Encourage the use of facial gestures and hand or body movements to get the message across. Explain to the pupils that this is not a mime. Can the class follow the clip? Why/why not?

Happy Birthday Rap

Ask the class if the 'Happy Birthday' song has met its used-by-date? It is often sung very badly anyway. Should it become a rap? Reset the 'Happy Birthday' song as a rap, adding some clicks and repetitions, and give it some actions. Watch all the raps and decide if they are an improvement. Select one or more for class birthdays.

A picture is worth a 1000 words

Read the following description to the pupils and at the end of it, ask them to draw an image that shows as much of the detail as possible.

- There was a very tall graceful tree that was losing its leaves. Its branches were like black lace. The old gnarled trunk was home to small creatures including an owl that lived in one of its many hollows.

Encourage the pupils to compare their pictures and to talk about the extra information that people added to their pictures.

Yes/No

This is a game that is played just like 'Round the world'. All the pupils must stand while waiting for their turn. On their turn the pupil must keep the yes/no pattern going, giving fresh new ideas each time. If they pass or repeat an idea, they are out and must sit down. The last person standing wins. Pick a topic such as, 'If someone has no lunch, should you share yours with them?'

The pupils follow the yes/no pattern as follows:
- Yes because the person will be hungry all day if you don't.
- No because if you do, you might be hungry all day.
- Yes because if you had no lunch, you would want someone to share their lunch with you.

Kung Fu Cheerleaders

Ask the pupils why they think teams of cheerleaders are not usually a mixture of boys and girls? What would a kung fu cheerleader's dance for boys and girls look like? What music and words would go with the new routine? Try out a few routines, present them to the school sports teams and see what they think.

The Most Adverbs

Provide a short basic starter sentence for the pupils to add to, for example, 'Tom walked to the shops.' Challenge the pupils to extend the sentence as far as possible, using only words that say how Tom walked to the shops. Model an example, such as 'Tom grumpily walked slowly and loudly dragging his feet to the shops.'

Repeat with a girl's name in the sentence before sharing and talking about the two sets of sentences. Discuss the sentences and differences in the stereotyping that arises.

In the style of?

For this activity the pupils first secretly choose a famous person, TV, book or cartoon character. They then decide how that character would respond to a particular situation, for instance, a child throwing a ball through a window or a bully teasing someone. They can then present a skit to demonstrate their character's response (including their accent). Ask the rest of the group or class to guess the character from the skit?

Mood Opposites

For this activity the pupils are going to show body language and facial gestures that are the opposite of what they are saying. For example they could act out anger as they try to tell someone how much they like them and want to be their friend. They could try to act out being happy as they tell a sad story. Ask the pupils to think of some of their own scenarios. Why is it hard to say 'No' when nodding 'Yes' with the head, or to look and sound exciting when you tell the world's most repeated joke?

Alphabet Stories

Divide the class into small groups. Have each group compose an alphabetical story that follows a proper story line with characters, setting, problem, twist and ending. In turn each pupil adds on a new word to the story so that the words follow in alphabetical order. A story might begin, 'After breakfast Claire decided everyone follow Graham home.' See how far the pupils get before they have to insert a word that breaks the alphabetical sequence. Penalties can apply for breaking the sequence. After a broken sequence the alphabet can continue either from the earlier word or from the first letter of the word that broke the sequence.

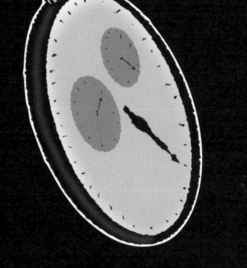

ACTIVITY BANK

NAME

Emoticon Graphs

What our class thinks about watching football on TV.

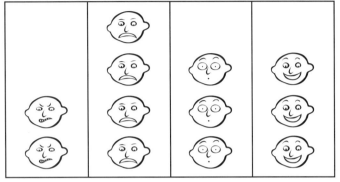

What might this graph be about? _____

What do the emoticon faces mean? _____

What information can you get from this graph? _____

Make an emoticon graph to show information you have collected from members of your class. You could ask about a particular food, pop group or TV show.

Do not label your graph yet. Ask your class first to predict what your graph is about and what it shows.

Mathematics: *interpreting, collecting and representing data.*

NAME

Buried Treasure

A game for 2 players.

Rules

Player 1 "buries" a treasure and secretly writes down its coordinates.

Player 2 asks a question (for example, Is it in E5?)

Player 1 answers:

"hot" if it is one square away in any direction, "warm" if it is two squares away in any direction, "cold" if it is three or more squares away in any direction.

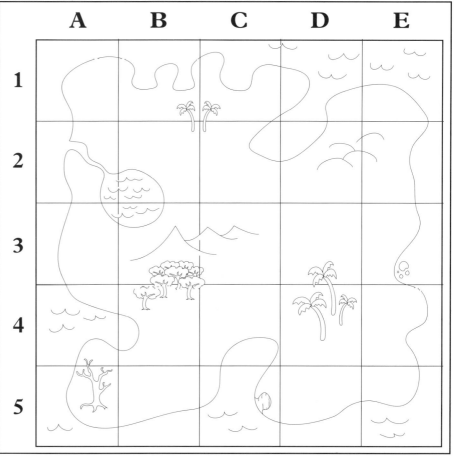

Player 2 wins if the square with the hidden treasure is found in 6 goes or less.

Play the game a few times.

What would be a good starting point to make sure that player 2 wins every time?

How could you change the rules to make a new game?

What if you played on a 7 by 7 grid?

Mathematics: *following directions with coordinates.*

NAME

Tracing Squares

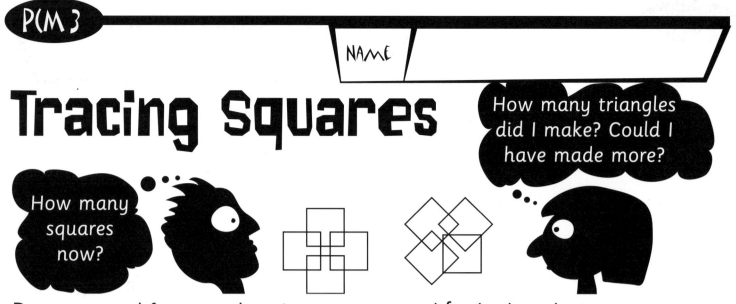

How many triangles did I make? Could I have made more?

How many squares now?

Draw around four overlapping squares and find what designs you can make?

Write interesting maths questions for your designs. Answer the questions before you give them to a friend to try.

Mathematics: *working with 2-D shapes.*

NAME

The Picnic

How many ants do you think are shown spoiling the picnic?

The illustrator has drawn the ants in special patterns to make them easy to count.

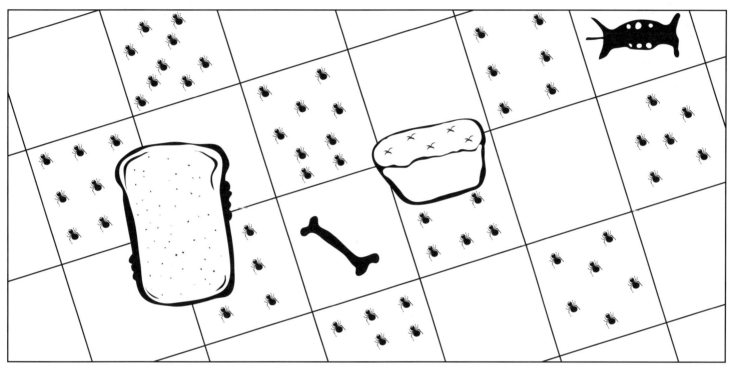

Show some of the easy patterns to count and describe the strategy you used for counting.

Show how you would work out how many ants there are altogether.

How many ants might be covered by the sandwich? Explain your thinking.

How many ants might be covered by the pie? _____

Explain your thinking. _____

Draw a picnic of your own. Set out the ants in ways that will make them easy for others to count.

Mathematics: *estimation and number strategies.*

NAME

Counting with Counters

How many counters do you think there are?

I estimate that the counter total is 1000. What do you think?

How could you work out the total for the counters altogether?

Could five people share the counters so that everyone gets the same total?

How would you work out the total for each person?

Which hand has the greatest counter total?

Make your own counter picture and write questions for it. Swap with a partner and work out the answers.

Mathematics: *using positional ideas and language.*

NAME

Land Sale

I bought 2 blocks and I have 16 trees.

I bought the first block to be sold and there were 45 trees left on the other blocks.

My 2 blocks have ¼ of the trees.

My block is in the NW corner.

My 2 blocks have 12 trees altogether.

Make up statements for four different buyers.
Make sure the number of trees works out.

Mathematics: *number and position.*

NAME

What's Inside the Egg?

Who is the mother? _____

Show the changes inside the egg day by day.

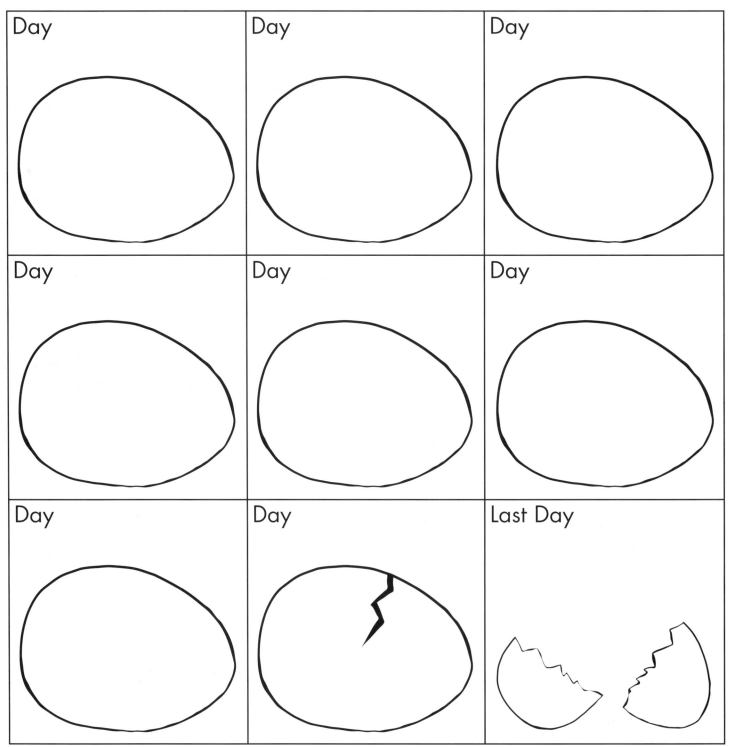

Day	Day	Day
Day	Day	Day
Day	Day	Last Day

Visual Literacy: *representing a sequence of events pictorially.*

NAME

The Dark and Stormy Night

Outside it was a dark stormy night.

Inside it was bright and cosy.

Use colour to contrast the outside mood and the inside mood.

Add any extra details you like.

Visual Literacy: *using colour to create mood and time.*

NAME

The Alphabet Playground

Make some larger than life letters.

Show how children could play on them.

Visual Literacy: *building on a visual stimulus.*

NAME

STORY BOARDS

Story boards show a story outline. Movie makers and illustrators use them to help them plan a sequence of pages or shots.

Close up
used to show emotions

Mid shot
used to show information about a person or place

Long shot
used to show what is happening

Complete the story board. Choose when to use a close up, mid shot or long shot. Think about the mood in each picture.

Little Miss Muffett sat on a tuffet eating her curds and whey.	There came a great spider...
Who sat down beside her...	And frightened Miss Muffett away.

Visual Literacy: *using framing and position to create a story board.*

NAME

How to Draw

The illustrator was supposed to create step-by-step instructions and diagrams for drawing a dog.

He's gone off on holiday. What do you think should be in each instruction box?

Visual Literacy: *creating instructions through diagrams only.*

NAME

Pattern Mania

As you can see, the artist did not get around to finishing this picture of pattern mania.

How would you finish it off? Fill every space with patterns.

Visual Literacy: *creating texture in illustration.*

NAME

Advertising Tricks

Colour the packet to help the advertiser sell this product.

The Healthy Breakfast Food for Growing Children

Mega Bites

It gives me lots of energy!

It's brain food!

A Balanced Diet

Recommended by Doctors

Ingredients
Sugar, fat, chocolate, colouring, preservatives, flour, glucose, salt.

Change the words and the colours used to create a packet that tells the truth.

Would anyone buy that cereal?
Why not?

Should advertisers be allowed to say things that are not really true?

Values: *understanding and questioning the ethics behind advertising.*

NAME

Bully or Victim?

Are the mice trying to bully and scare the elephant or
is he just being a silly victim? Can mice really hurt him?

Help! Help! MICE!

Create your own bully and victim picture.

What is the bully doing? Who is the victim?

Does the victim need to be afraid?
What could the victim do to stop being a victim?

Values: *exploring relationship issues.*

NAME

The Chameleon

When a chameleon does not want to be noticed, it changes its colour to match the surroundings.
Some creatures and some people too do not want to be noticed.

Complete the pictures below to show living creatures that can blend in with their backgrounds. Make up one of your own.

Why do we sometimes want to be unnoticed?

_____

What could you do to overcome your shyness?

_____

Values: *understanding personal behaviours.*

NAME

Why did the Leopard Change its Spots?

Complete the comic strip to explain why the leopard changed its spots and why it still wasn't happy.

The leopard always hid in the same spot waiting for its prey.  **I wish I had tiger stripes**	Then one day...
Now it wasn't spotty anymore. It was  _____	It wasn't happy though, because _____

So _____

Values: *accepting and valuing difference.*

NAME

How Embarrassing!

Why don't you tie your sweatshirt round your waist?

I hope they can't see my Spider Man underpants.

I'll have to walk backwards.

Now they'll tease me for ever.

Look everyone, he's split his trousers. Ha ha ha ha ha!

Why do people get so embarrassed?

Is it okay to embarrass people?

Should we really laugh at people when something embarrassing happens?

Should the children have told him about the split in his trousers?

Create an embarrassing moment and show how to handle it in the most embarrassing way.

Now show how to make it a less embarrassing situation.

Values: *developing empathy and respect for others.*

NAME

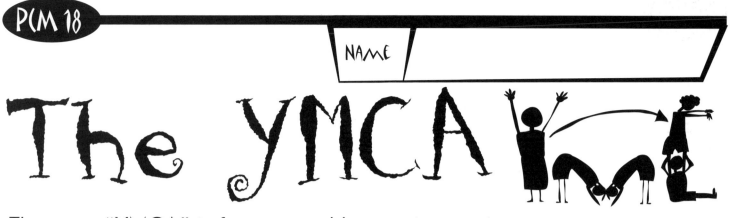

The YMCA

The song "YMCA" is famous and has actions to it.

Have you noticed how smoothly dancers move from one position to another? Well it's your job to be nice and smooth as you and two friends form the letters of the song "YMCA" as smoothly as can be.

Show how the three of you will make each letter.

Music and Dance: *choreographing simple movement sequences.*

NAME

THE OPPOSITES DANCE

high-low

fast-slow

left-right

The steps

For this dance you and your partner move around in a circle. You and your partner always do the opposite. So if one goes fast around the circle, the other goes slowly around the circle till you meet again.

Try out the dance shown above. Then make up an opposites dance of your own.

Draw and/or list your dance steps and actions, in sequence, here.

What music will you use in the background to match your dance?

Rehearse and then perform your dance.

Music and Dance: *working together to create opposites through movement.*

NAME

Slip, Slop, Slap

(Slip 3 left)
Slip, slip, slip
On a hat

(Slop face three
times)
Slop, slop, slop
on sunscreen

(Slap, turn slap
on a hat)
Slap, slap
slappity hat

(Slip 3 right)
Slip, slop, slap
Join in the rap

Create a dance and jingle with actions for a TV advert.
Rehearse so you can present it later. Keep in time and stay together.

Perform the advert for your class.

Music and Dance: *conveying a message through dance and music.*

NAME

The Human Band

We can pop or roll our lips and blow.

Join with two or three friends to create a human band.

Experiment with musical body noises.

We can clap or click our fingers.

We can stamp our feet.

Each of you pick a noise to make. Follow the sequence below, coming in where the diagram shows you to.

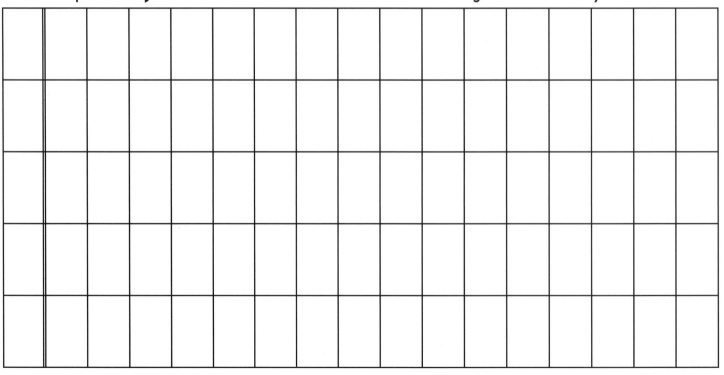

Now create your own repeating rhythm with body noises.

Make up a sequence chart so that the class can join in with you.

Music: *exploring rhythm and sound.*

NAME

Secret Messages

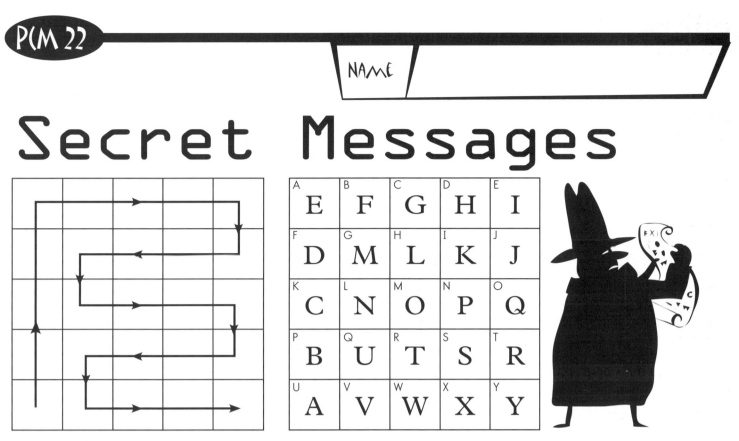

A	B	C	D	E
E	F	G	H	I
F	G	H	I	J
D	M	L	K	J
K	L	M	N	O
C	N	O	P	Q
P	Q	R	S	T
B	U	T	S	R
U	V	W	X	Y
A	V	W	X	Y

To make this secret code chart, I made a path on the grid.

Then I began at the beginning of the path and wrote the letters of the alphabet in order as I followed the path.

The alphabet used for cracking the code is written in sequence in smaller letters. It starts at the top left as usual.

What does this message say?   **OY GER LES DNIES**

Make up a new path on the grid. Write the alphabet as you follow the path.

Write the same message in the new code.

A	B	C	D	E
F	G	H	I	J
K	L	M	N	O
P	Q	R	S	T
U	V	W	X	Y

Communication: *communicating in secret code.*

NAME

Make the *Bird*

Complete the instructions for making this bird.
Remember to say what materials are used and
when to join things on. You are given a few hints.

Step 1.
Make a large plasticine
ball for the body.

Step 2.

Step 3.

Step 4.

Step 5.

Step 6.

Step 7.

Step 8.

Step 9.

Create a character of your own. List the materials needed to make it.
Create the instructions for it. Can your partner follow your instructions?

Communication: *creating a verbal and visual procedural text.*

NAME

The Great Escape

The dog is locked in the garden and wants to get out to join his friends. He'll never get out.

But wait, here he is later in the day. He is out with the other dogs. How did he do it?

Please show what he did and explain how he got out.
I bet his owners will not be happy.

Communication: *explaining a situation to others.*

NAME

Talk About Strange

Is it true?

I wonder what it looks like?

Is it the Loch Ness Monster?

The Daily Bungle

Man catches a Giant Dragon Fish Never Seen Before.

How did they catch it?

Does it live at the bottom of the ocean?

Create thought bubbles for the headline below.

Mad Dog Runs Wild at Supermarket.

Share with a partner what you wrote. Do they have similar ideas?
Why do you have similar ideas?
Why do you have ideas that are very different?
Where did the ideas come from?

Communication: *responding verbally and creatively to headlines.*

Spin a Yarn

Well that was not very interesting and there was not enough information. See his second go at spinning a yarn.

Suddenly everyone is interested and has lots of questions.
Use a highlighter pen to mark the parts you think make the yarn interesting.

Spin an interesting yarn of your own. Share it with the class.
How will you grab their attention?

Communication: *creating and telling an interesting yarn.*

NAME

Text, Text, Text

Type this as a text message: See you at eight at the park and we can kick a ball together. See you later.

C U @ 8 @ the park and we can kick a ball 2gether. C U L8ter.

Is this what you typed?

Gr8 C U by 4 now.

What does the reply say?

Write a message long hand.

Write the message text style here.

Show only the text message to your friends. Can they read it?

Will all writing be like text message writing in the future?
Give reasons for your opinions.

Communication: *communicating in SMS format.*

CHALLENGES

TASK CARD 1 — Chinese Whispers

What you need:

- pencil and paper
- 5 or 6 friends

What to do:

Rules for "Chinese Whispers"

Whisper a message to a friend who whispers it to another friend and so on at least 4 or 5 times, until the message comes back to you. Usually the message that comes back is very different to the message that began the chain.

Now, write down a message one or two sentences long.

Write down the changes you predict might happen as the message is passed on.

Play the game and see what happens.

Think about why messages get changed. Is it because of unclear pronunciation, listening skills, short-term memory issues, lack of concentration or other factors?

Is it possible to get to the stage where a message goes around clearly?

TASK CARD 2 — Bottle Top Towers

What you need:

- 20 plastic bottle tops
- pencil and paper

What to do:

Your task is to build the highest tower you can such that every layer of the tower is bigger than the one underneath.

Keep a record of what you try, and what does and doesn't work.

When you think you have the largest top storey possible, create the instructions with diagrams so that a friend can build it too.

TASK CARD 3

The Maths Trail

What you need:

- pencil and paper
- ruler or tape measure
- kitchen or bathroom scales
- containers of small objects (buttons, counters, lollies)

What to do:

Your task is to create a class maths trail that includes questions about:

- measuring the distance or length of an object
- finding something of a given mass
- guessing how many of something in a container
- guessing how many of something will fit in a container
- finding something that is smaller but heavier than an object you chose.

A question might be: There is something in this room that has a mass the same as this book but it is only about a quarter of its size. What is it?

Write the answers somewhere secret.

Give your trail to a friend and make sure they estimate and then check.

TASK CARD 4

Do I Look Good?

What you need:

- pencil and paper
- dress up clothes or costumes
- 3 or 4 friends

What to do:

Your task is to create a scripted skit (3 minutes long) about someone asking if they look good in their costume. Your skit must show the hidden thinking about whether to lie or whether to tell the truth, and what the consequences of telling the truth or not telling the truth would be.

Rehearse and perform your skit to the class. Ask them to give feedback on what they thought of the issues you raised in the skit and what was good about your skit.

Make and Take

What you need:

- scrap materials (boxes, cylinders, paper, card, string)
- glue
- paint
- pencil and paper
- ice-cream container
- sand pit or sand tray

What to do:

Make a model that will pick up sand and deposit it in the ice cream container.

Create the instructions for your device.

Invite a friend to come to a make and take where they make the model from your instructions and the materials that you have ready for them.

How good were your instructions? Revise them and test them on another friend.

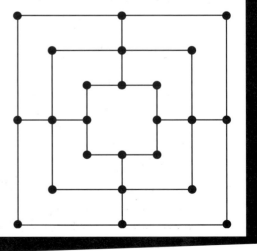

Three Men's Morris

What you need:

- pencil and paper
- ruler
- 6 counters in two colours (3 of each colour)
- a partner

What to do

Two players take turns to place each of their counters anywhere on the board. Players then take turns to slide one of their counters to a new spot on the board without jumping over any counters. The first player to have three counters in a straight line, diagonally, vertically or horizontally on the board wins the game.

Find a way to record the moves for a game so that you can investigate whether there are some good starting moves. Select one set of starting moves and then investigate what is the least number of moves possible for a player to win.